Bruce SPRINGSTEEN

by Keith Elliot Greenberg

Lerner Publications Company
Minneapolis

Photo Credits

Steve Rapport/London Features International, p. 4; Jodi Summers Dorland/Retna, pp. 8, 30; Nancy Barr, pp.1, 11, 14, 16, 22, 26, 29; US/MP/London Features International, p.20.

Front cover photo by Larry Busacca/Retna
Back cover photo by Rocky Widner/Retna

Manufactured in the United States of America

LIBRARY OF CONGRESS CATALOGING-IN-PUBLICATION DATA

Greenberg, Keith Elliot.
  Bruce Springsteen.

  Summary: Follows the life and career of the popular performer, hailed as "The Boss" of rock and roll music.
  1. Springsteen, Bruce—Juvenile literature. 2. Rock musicians—United States—Biography—Juvenile literature. [1. Springsteen, Bruce. 2. Musicians. 3. Rock music] I. Title.
ML3930.S72G7 1986   784.5'4'00924 [B] [92]   85-18035
ISBN 0-8225-1608-X (lib. bdg.)

1 2 3 4 5 6 7 8 9 10 96 95 94 93 92 91 90 89 88 87 86

Contents

American Hero 5

Growing Up 9

Making It 17

The "Bruce Juice" Explosion 21

Never Forgetting 27

The Future 31

American Hero

Bruce Springsteen is an American hero. Like the revolutionaries who founded this country, he believes in taking action to change the things he doesn't like. While the revolutionaries took action by waging war, the peaceful Springsteen uses his songs, his words, and his contributions to various charities to improve the world's condition.

When Bruce, also known as "The Boss," sings from the heart, working people everywhere can relate. Every adult has probably lived his simple stories of love and labor and met the colorful characters in his tales. Many years from now, when historians want to see what America was like during our time, Bruce's music will provide the answer.

Bruce shows real concern for his fans. He tells his listeners to be true to themselves. At one concert, he spoke to his audience about the dangers of "blind faith." He warned against trusting anybody or anything without question, "whether it's....your girlfriend or the government."

Although people are quick to hail him as a sort of prophet, Bruce also tells his fans not to have blind faith in him. "Trust the art, not the artist," he said. "I think somebody can do real good work and be a fool in a variety of ways. I think my music is probably better than I am. I mean, like, your music is your ideals a lot of times and you don't live up to those ideals all the time. You try, but you fall short."

He realizes that people are spending their hard-earned money to buy his records and attend his concerts, and he tries to give them their dollars' worth. While other artists consider forty minutes on stage a show, Bruce rarely leaves the stage until he has performed for at least three hours. In the course of a concert, he loses between three and five pounds.

Away from the stage and the studio, Bruce sets a healthy example. He stays away from drugs, works out in the gym, and is generally polite. When he first met his wife's parents, they were surprised at the rock star's humble behavior. "They were delighted," said a friend of the family. "Bruce was very quiet and subdued, didn't smoke or drink. They were also pleased to hear that Bruce gives money to charities in every city he performs in."

Because so many people think so highly of Bruce Springsteen, politicians have quoted him to gain popular favor. President Ronald Reagan mentioned Bruce's song "Born in the U.S.A." during the 1984 presidential campaign. After eleven fans were trampled to death at a 1979 Who concert in Cincinnati, Ohio, the mayor of that city, Jerry Springer, pointed at the well-behaved audiences at Springsteen concerts and stated that rock'n'roll was not to blame for the tragedy. "Bruce Springsteen showed us that," the mayor said, "and we should be grateful to him."

Bruce Springsteen has been called many things, from the king of rock'n'roll to the greatest performer of the twentieth century. But the most accurate description of him — and the true definition of an American hero — came from the lips of his sister-in-law, Mary Lepschaut. Bruce Springsteen, she said, is "a real down-to-earth guy."

Growing Up

Bruce Springsteen was born on September 23, 1949, in Freehold, New Jersey, a working-class town fifteen miles away from the beach-front communities the singer would one day make famous. Bruce's mother, Adele, was Italian and came from a family of great storytellers. Bruce's father, Douglas, was Dutch and Irish. There were two other children in the family, Bruce's younger sisters, Ginny and Pam.

Douglas Springsteen was always struggling to make a living; he worked as a prison guard, a factory worker, and a bus driver. It was from Douglas that Bruce developed the love for the road that would inspire so many songs.

Both father and son were stubborn, and they often clashed. Bruce was very independent-minded and he didn't like following his father's rules. The boy also had problems obeying the strict priests and nuns in parochial school. Because he was quiet and didn't always dress and act the same as the other kids, some of Bruce's classmates said he was "weird."

Bruce felt aimless until he discovered rock music. He first became introduced to rock'n'roll when he saw Elvis Presley on *The Ed Sullivan Show.* Springsteen remembered, "Man, when I was nine, I couldn't imagine anyone *not* wanting to be Elvis Presley." When he was 13, his parents bought him a guitar in a pawn shop for $18. Suddenly, things were looking up for Bruce Springsteen.

"I know that rock'n'roll changed my life," he said. "It was something for me to hold on to.... It really gave me a sense of myself, and it allowed me to become useful, which I think most people want to be."

His love for music kept him away from drugs. "I never did any drugs," Bruce said. "When I was at the age when it was popular.... I was practicing in my room with my guitar."

By the time he started high school, Bruce's favorite recording artists included Elvis, Chuck Berry, the Beatles, the Rolling Stones, Eric Burdon and the Animals, Manfred Mann, the Who, Sam Cooke, Mitch Ryder, the

Rascals, Martha and the Vandellas, Roy Orbison, and a dynamic kid from Norfolk, Virginia, named Gary U.S. Bonds. Bruce desperately wanted to get into a band like the Castiles, a group of teenagers who practiced in Freehold. A stroke of luck came his way when the band's rhythm guitarist, George Theiss, got a crush on Ginny Springsteen and, in an effort to charm the girl, asked her brother to audition for the Castiles. The enthusiastic Springsteen easily passed.

Bruce's high school graduation picture. He said of himself "I was quiet and shy and liked to putter with cars."

Bruce performed at the Yellow Futz coffeehouse in Sea Bright, New Jersey in the early 70s.

The Castiles were managed by Tex Vinyard, a thirty-two-year-old factory worker who allowed the boys to rehearse in his home. Tex and his wife, Marion, had no children of their own and took a special interest in the local teenagers. Besides managing several groups, the couple put twelve youths through college and were always around to offer personal and musical advice. Bruce affectionately calls the Vinyards "the Mom and Pop of rock on the Jersey shore."

Tex booked the group to play dances at schools, teen clubs, roller rinks, and swim clubs. They played at the grand opening of a supermarket and at a drive-in theater before the showing of a film. They were extremely popular and creative; Bruce surprised followers one time by performing indoors on a lifeguard tower. Towards the end of Bruce's high school career, the band played a few dates in the Greenwich Village section of New York City, which at the time was bursting with groups on the verge of national fame. The Castiles were never offered a recording contract, however, and the band broke up after Bruce graduated from high school.

Bruce "wanted to go further with his music," Tex recalled. He began hanging out with other musicians at boardwalk clubs in Asbury Park, New Jersey. His groups had names like Earth, Child, and Steel Mill, and the musicians he played with — Southside Johnny Lyons, Miami Steve Van Zandt, Garry W. Tallent — would eventually perform beside him in the country's big arenas. Besides being a haven for musicians, Asbury Park was filled with odd-ball characters — fortune tellers, pinball kings and beachcomber Romeos — about whom Bruce wrote songs.

In 1969, Douglas Springsteen relocated the family to California. Bruce chose to remain in New Jersey, living with friends and trying to make a living as a musician. His band, Steel Mill, was now a favorite at rock clubs and colleges all over the northeastern coast. When the group toured San Francisco, a company there offered them a recording contract. They rejected it because very little money went along with it. Still, Bruce was confident that he could achieve everything he wanted in life if he stuck to his principles and continued playing rock'n'roll.

After Steel Mill broke up, Bruce formed a band called Dr. Zoom and the Sonic Boom. The format of the group was loose, to say the least. When the band played, there was a Monopoly table set up in the middle of the stage. "That was to give people who didn't play anything a chance to be in the band," Bruce laughed. "You know, so they could say, 'Yeah, I'm in Dr. Zoom. I play Monopoly.'"

Next came a unit known as the Bruce Springsteen Band, composed of many of the Asbury Park regulars.

One night, when they were taking a break outdoors, Bruce and band member Miami Steve Van Zandt ran into Clarence "The Big Man" Clemons, a saxophone player who was taking a break from playing at a nearby club. Bruce discovered that he and Clemons, a six-foot, four-inch former college football player, had many

13

Clarence "The Big Man" Clemons and Bruce have been good friends onstage and off since they first met.

things in common. Besides sharing musical tastes, both were concerned about the underprivileged; when he wasn't performing, Clarence was a social worker for young children. A deep friendship was quickly formed between the two men.

Because the Bruce Springsteen Band was making very little money, the group broke up. But word of Bruce's talent spread. A meeting was set up between the performer and John Hammond, a record company executive who discovered legendary folk singer Bob Dylan and jazz great Benny Goodman. When Bruce played a song for him, Hammond was impressed. "I knew at once that [Springsteen] would last a generation," he said.

Bruce was signed to CBS Records on June 9, 1972.

Making It

Bruce contacted a few of his Asbury Park buddies and asked them to play on his first album. Although his special talents had gotten him the recording contract, he wanted the gifted musicians he had struggled with to be heard as well. Instead of calling his act just "Bruce Springsteen," he called it "Bruce Springsteen *and* The E Street Band," after a street in Asbury Park.

Bruce's first album, *Greetings From Asbury Park, New Jersey*, released in January, 1973, lived up to its title. Listening to the record, one could practically hear the clanging of the pinball arcades, see the neon of the amusement park, and smell the cotton candy and popcorn of the boardwalk. Bruce established himself as a great poet, writing about such universal themes as romance, mischief, and a sense of belonging. One song, "Growing Up," told of the performer's awkward childhood and battle to follow his beliefs.

The publicity department at CBS records portrayed Bruce as a new Bob Dylan. Although Bruce saw certain similarities — Dylan also was a master wordsmith, and his songs reflected the anger of the younger generation — he grew to resent the comparison. He preferred being known as his own person, rather than a modern-day version of somebody else.

During the tour to promote the album, Bruce astounded new fans by staying on stage longer than most acts, and talking sincerely to his audience between songs. He said that it was important for the musician and his audience to "support each other." "Some guy bought his ticket and there's a promise made between the musician and the audience.... It goes real deep.... If you break the pact or take it too lightly, nothing else makes sense. It's at the heart of everything."

The reason people respond the way they do to rock 'n' roll, Bruce said, is that they see themselves in the music. At the same time, he continued, a musician should be able to look at the fans and see himself.

The Wild, The Innocent & The E Street Shuffle,

18

Bruce's second album, told more rich tales about life in Asbury Park and the difficulty of growing up. Critics generally liked it, and Bruce said the album helped perfect his style. "On the second album, I started slowly to find out who I am and where I wanted to be," he said. "It was like coming out . . . . and trying to be yourself."

On one song, "Rosalita," Bruce tells of a girl whose parents don't want her to date a rocker. The rocker proves the parents wrong when he becomes a success and is able to provide a good life for the girl. This was clearly Bruce singing about the freedom he gained through rock 'n' roll, and anybody who had ever had dreams considered "far-out" by others could empathize.

In fact, so many people could empathize with Springsteen that rock critic Jon Landau predicted, "I saw rock and roll's future and its name is Bruce Springsteen."

The "Bruce Juice" Explosion

By the time Bruce went into the studio to record *Born to Run*, the E Street Band was tighter than it had ever been, with Clarence Clemons on saxophone, Garry W. Tallent on bass guitar, Roy Bittan on piano, Danny Federici on organ, Max Weinberg on drums, and Miami Steve Van Zandt singing background vocals and doing horn arrangements. Besides singing, Bruce played the guitar and the harmonica.

Work on the album took longer than expected because

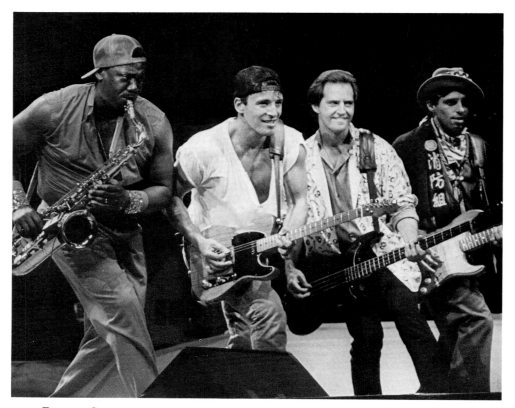

Bruce Springsteen and his band walked right into stardom. Left to right, Clarence Clemons, Bruce, Garry Tallent, and Nils Lofgren (Miami Steve Van Zandt's replacement).

Bruce had difficulty getting down on tape the sound he heard in his head when he wrote the music. Finally, he called music critic Jon Landau for help. Landau quit his writing job, and co-produced the album. The rough spots were ironed out, and *Born to Run*, released in 1975, became one of the best-selling albums of the 1970s.

The title song was an anthem to romance, fast cars, and youthful dreams. Other tunes dealt with values concerning friendship and faith. Bruce's young listeners, who frequently requested that radio stations play more "Bruce Juice" (their special term for Springsteen's music), said he spoke for their generation. Newspapers and magazines began examining his popularity, and on October 27, 1975, he appeared on the covers of both *Time* and *Newsweek*, a spot normally reserved for world leaders.

Bruce refused to let fame change him. He tried extra hard not to lose touch with his fans. In every town he toured, he paid close attention to the people, their hopes, and fears, and their likes and dislikes. Of course, as he traveled, he met all sorts of interesting individuals who would one day appear in his songs.

His next two albums, *Darkness on the Edge of Town* (1978), and *The River* (1980), were segments of a three-part story that began with *Born to Run*. The characters on *Born to Run* were full of energy and plans for the future. On *Darkness on the Edge of Town*, they tried dealing with the problems of the real world. On *The River*, they offered comfort to one another over life's difficulties.

Instead of following *The River* with another album featuring his now-renowned E Street Band, Bruce went back to his musical roots and played simple acoustic guitar on his next record, *Nebraska*. Acclaimed by the critics as "brilliant," *Nebraska*, released in 1982, was filled with eerie songs of loneliness.

Bruce didn't tour after *Nebraska* was released, and he tried to find other things to occupy the time usually spent on the road. Phil Dunphy, a trainer, suggested that Bruce join a gym and begin working on his body. Bruce took Phil's advice. At 5'10" and 155 pounds, the singer now has an athlete's build, and he runs six miles every day.

In 1984, *Born in the U.S.A.* came out and quickly soared to the top of the music charts. The title song is the story of a kid who gets drafted, goes to Vietnam, and comes back to people who don't understand or appreciate him. Yet he still loves America and American rock'n'roll. Many of the songs on the album ("Darlington County," "Working on the Highway," "Downbound Train," "I'm on Fire," "Bobby Jean," "My Hometown," and "Glory Days") were recorded live and allow the listener to share the excitement of a Springsteen concert.

Special "dance" versions of two other tunes, "Dancing in the Dark" and "Cover Me," have also been released. Bruce made the decision to have these songs re-mixed into dance singles in the studio after he heard the "dance mix" version of Cyndi Lauper's "Girls Just Want to Have Fun." "It was incredible," he said. "It sounded like fun."

Born in the U.S.A. is Bruce's first album from which videos were made. "Video is a powerful thing," he said, "and I wanted to be involved in it in some fashion."

Video has helped Bruce win new fans. "I was on the beach," the performer happily recalled, "and this kid came up to me — I think his name was Mike, he was like seven or eight — and he says, 'I saw you on MTV.' And then he says, 'I got your [dance] moves down.' So I say, 'Well, let me check 'em out.' And he starts [dancing]. And he was *pretty good*, you know?"

Never Forgetting

There were many people who helped Bruce climb to stardom, from his family to his musician friends to various record company executives. Bruce is very conscious of not forgetting them. "The danger of fame is forgetting," he said.

Through the years, Bruce has helped other musicians with their projects. He often appeared on stage with his Asbury Park buddy, Southside Johnny Lyons, and Johnny's band, The Jukes. When Clarence Clemons made a solo album, Bruce was around for assistance. Former E Street Band member Miami Steve Van Zandt produced *The River* and *Born in the U.S.A.* — at Bruce's request. Since he went solo, Miami Steve has been replaced by legendary guitarist Nils Lofgren. John Cafferty, whose Beaver Brown Band provided the soundtrack for the rock film, *Eddie and the Cruisers*, has known Bruce since the early 1970s. He said, "Bruce would give me a lot of encouragement, a lot of advice. He helped me find a lot of answers concerning songwriting."

After one of Bruce's childhood idols, Gary U.S. Bonds, dropped out of the public eye, he was approached by a brown-haired fan in a New Jersey cocktail lounge. Gary didn't realize that the fan was Bruce Springsteen. Bruce wanted to help Gary get his career started again. Springsteen wrote three songs for Gary's album, *Dedication*. The E Street Band backed up Gary's singing, and Bruce paid for the studio time his hero could not afford. Almost twenty years after his last hit, Gary U.S. Bonds was playing sell-out shows again.

Bruce has not forgotten the needy people outside the music industry either. He contributes to charities all over the world. He participated in the "No Nukes" concerts at New York's Madison Square Garden, dedicated to preventing nuclear war. With forty-four other performers, he recorded the song, "We Are The World" as part of the "U.S.A. For Africa" effort. All money made from the record's sales was donated to organizations bringing food to starving Africans.

Born in the U.S.A. was written for the American veterans of the Vietnam War. Many of Bruce's childhood

The "No Nukes" benefit concert is one of many Bruce has given his time and talent to. Here he performed with Jackson Browne and Tom Petty.

friends served in Vietnam, and the Castiles' drummer, Bart Hanes, was killed there. Bruce wants the frequently misunderstood Vietnam veterans to be remembered as heroes. "There was a moment when they were just really generous with their lives," he said.

Knowing this, Bruce has not forgotten to be generous to the war's survivors.

The Future

Bruce Springsteen has gone from being just another dreamer with a guitar to an internationally-known celebrity. In May of 1985, Bruce began his European tour by leading 100,000 fans in singing "Born in the U.S.A." at Ireland's historic Slane Castle. Two other rock giants, Pete Townshend of The Who and Eric Clapton, joined him on stage.

There is no doubt that Bruce will continue to tour and bring his musical stories and messages to his increasing number of followers. Now that he is married to model Julianne Phillips, he plans to spend a little more time at home, though. He plans to find a farm with a big barn that he can convert into a studio. That way, he will be able to record without traveling.

He wants a family. He has said that "the things that I admire and the things that mean a lot to me all have to do with roots and home.... I see fulfillment, ultimately, in family life."

Most probably, Bruce will do what he has always done and put his new experiences to music. He may be getting older, but he still knows how to communicate with his fans. Because of that, he will be considered an American hero for many years to come.